Fears to Feathers

Ruth Glendinning

BookLeaf
Publishing

India | USA | UK

Presentation by *BookLeaf Publishing*

Web: www.bookleafpub.com

E-mail: info@bookleafpub.com

ISBN: 9789358318944

First edition 2023

DEDICATION

This collection of poems is dedicated to all those who are ready to find their wings, take that leap of faith, and fly into the future.

The world is waiting for you.

ACKNOWLEDGEMENT

First and foremost, I want to thank my parents, Margaret Downs and Walter Glendinning, both of whom are now in spirit, for seeding a lifelong love for language in me. I took that passion for words and built a flourishing garden of ideas in which the poems became the transformative flowers that bloom throughout so much of my writing.

A lifetime of gratitude to Mike Rose, my dear friend, mentor and a huge fan of poetry, who is also in spirit now. He was thrilled that I had 'found my voice' and was using it to bring my vision of an equitable, accessible, inclusive world to fruition.

Finally, one thing writers absolutely cannot do without is readers. I have been quite fortunate to have folks who have read and/or listened to me recite each word of these poems. Deep thanks to Susan Wenck, Kent Dahlgren, Sophie Beilinson, Bonnie Glendinning, Connie Mongreig, Mark Wojton and many others. Their ongoing support gives me the confidence to continue to share the work.

Special thanks to Trudy Martinez for her encouragement, editing talent and support on this journey.

PREFACE

The title of this volume came from a mantra inspired by one of the poems:

"She transformed her fears to feathers
and flew into the future."

This has become a mantra for me as I experience my own journey in mind, body and spirit to the imagined world of what's next.

We're living in a time of change, in which we have the opportunity to reframe the story of the future. Language is our most valuable technology because, without it, we cannot express thoughts, or invite others into our shared dream of what can be.

I have found poetry to hold a special magic, opening others to the idea that language can be both playful and profound, speaking volumes in a few words and reminding us of who else we are.

May we all find our wings and fly into our future dreams.

Releasing the Secrets

Another a-ha, another leap
Off the ledge, into the deep

Immersing in the unremembered
Considering the unexpected beauty tendered

The softness of the landing
Floating more than standing

No longer in limbo
Wings spread, arms akimbo

Joining the winged creatures in the sky
Seeing the world anew from on high

Following the path of the soaring birds
Slowly discovering new songs and words

Singing along with the tune on the breeze
Our destination peeks through the trees

Following the thread of color and light
The curve of the land matches the arc of flight

Watching the words drop to the ground
What was lost has now been found

The blank pages of the new tale are filling
The rise and fall of the voices are thrilling

No longer apart from the chorus
We follow our souls through the forest

Seeking our place among the others
Our long-lost, dreamed-of sisters and brothers

The secret stardust begins to glow
Illuminating the twilight shadow

Into the new story unfolding
Releasing the secrets we have been holding

Leaning in closer feeling the unwinding
Fears fall away, no longer binding

Our hearts and souls free at last
Celebrating the future and releasing the past

Reminding All

May you live a life of wildness and wonder
And never fear of being taken asunder

From the threads connecting you to others
The seen and unseen sisters and brothers

All a part of an unending galaxy of faith
Delicately holding our truth in place

The truth is that we have a sacred duty
To plant the seeds of future beauty

To share our stardust for all to see
Illuminating the path from me to we

Awakening the sleeping flowers
Activating their delicate powers

To attract the butterflies and bees to the dance
Saving the world with the ancient romance

Between them and us and all we see
To become all that we can be

As part of the story written so long ago
A complex weave of Light and Shadow

A perfect balance of heaven and earth
Each thread binding us to our true worth

Onward to the depths of the darkest forest
Our voices rising as we join Gaia's chorus

Each note sharing our inner stardust
Building in strength and deepening trust

We are all here because we have been there
Reminding all that it's time to care

Feeling the Truth

My dear, my darling, my love, myself
It's time to take the book off the shelf

To invoke the message waiting inside
That our need for truth is stronger than pride

It's upon us to protect the light bringers
And hear the words of the truth singers

To seek those whose gift is to see
Who else we were born to be

What else this world can become
When we share the light of the ancient sun

What can the flowers teach us about blooming
What cloth are the weavers looming

How do we follow our soul's compass
Surrendering to faith we can reach Oneness

Each playing a part in the story unfolding
Adding the secrets each have been holding

Understanding the secrets have been holding us

Silent and breathless fearful of fuss

Bound by false stories with loose tethers
Exhaling and transforming fears to feathers

To leap off the edge, following the birds
Feeling the truth in the remembered words

That we are in this moment, in this place
To leave fears behind and move with grace

Into the world where there is no other
Reconnected as sister and brother

Awakening Hearts and Minds

The messages delivered by the smallest bird
The words were spoken, but remained unheard

Until the curious folks listened with their heart
Understood that it was time to start

The old story was finally flickering out
It's time for a new tale, she said with a shout

Gathering the millions of words from the ground
Purposely dropped by the birds to be found

When spoken they transformed into seeds
Releasing the truths the world now needs

Each seed becomes a flower
Speaking truth to power

Awakening hearts and minds
Breaking the trance that binds

The world to a false story
That we are not worthy of glory

Or to ascend to the skies above
Aloft on wings of love

Sharing the skies with the birds
Exclaiming the magical words

That we are all more than enough
That we all are made of the right stuff

To create a world that works for all
To be unafraid of answering the call

Recognizing the truth in ourselves and others
That we are all sisters and brothers

Souls of a feather
We rise together

Flying high under the warmth of the sun
Spreading the news that the new story has begun

Carrying the Message

It was the first bird of the morning
The flutter of wings began without warning

Carrying the message that needed to be heard
The story of future was brought by that bird

Singing the tales of lives not yet discovered
With each note our souls were recovered

The flame teased from the scattered embers
The mind forgets what the heart remembers

We are not here to rage and destroy
Our purpose is not to treat the Earth as a toy

It is to find the magic in ourselves and others
The truth is we're sisters and brothers

It is to remember the present is truly a gift
And strength should be used to give others a lift

Unbound from the false construct of time
Leaning into truth powerful and sublime

That there are no limits to our story while here
We just keep breathing and rising above fear

Proof of our faith is shown at the edge
Across the chasm and into the verdant sedge

There are only futures now remembered
Awakened by the birds, stirring the embers

Illuminated by the fire in our eyes
We spread our wings and take to the skies

Seeking the Source

Exhaling her fear she took the leap
Over the edge with one giant sweep

Into the gap between here and there
Exulting in the freedom beyond compare

Flying through the air on new wings
She floated along observing all the things

The world was different from up on high
Here with the birds in the sky

Released from the cocoon she called home
The sounds from below had a complex tone

Following the perfume wafting from the flowers
Tapping into these new mystical powers

Seeking the source of the intoxicating scent
She began a slow spiraling descent

The world around her shifted from blue to green
Reminding her of what else she had been

Before emerging in this new glory

Perspective framed by a different story

She wondered if others know how they are seen
Before they wake up from their dream

Do they still believe they're what they had been
Or do they sense a change in the Golden Mean

Souls arise and threads come unwound
We're all choosing to spiral up or to spiral down

The well-worn path or the road less traveled
The future is ours, with the past unraveled

Leaping into the story that feeds our soul
Awakening the dreamers, it's time to go

Finding the Others

An ode to the mother
The unseen other

Planting the seeds of future
Using the threads of the past to suture

Broken dreams
And torn seams

Patching the hole
Making us whole

Turning fears into feathers
Untying the binding tethers

Releasing us on our journey to now
Carrying the why, discovering the how

To be our own mothers
And finding the others

Through shadows and light
Engaging our souls' wings for flight

Away from what was, towards what can be
No longer alone, finding our we

Becoming…

The mother of all and none
The mother of many and one

The mother of future and past
The mother of the answer and the ask

The mother of what can be
Released at last in you and me

Binding Her to a False Story

She woke to see the cage door hanging akimbo
The caged bird no longer caught in limbo

Just a soft bit of color, a tiny feather
Indicating where it had slipped its tether

A single note drew attention to the horizon
She watched to see if she could lay her eyes on

The small bird that had embodied hope
That had now shown her how to slip the rope

Binding her to a false story of herself
Dusty and worn, like a book on a shelf

It was time for her to follow that bird
To raise her voice and say the word

That would free her from the fluttering fears
That had kept her bound all these years

It was time to jump, to take the leap
To release with joy the secrets you keep

To surrender to faith, that awaits your command
And turn your eyes to the unfolding land

Over the edge and into the air
Wings emerge, expanding with grace and flair

The game has changed, the race is on
To find the bird carrying Gaia's song

Off she flew into parts unknown
Her soul telling her she was flying home

Back to the place from whence she came
Where she learned the true rules to the game

Of life and love and all that entails
The joy and grief of wins and fails

The quest for wisdom and truth
Believing in both without any proof

This is where the journey began once again
For this soldier of Gaia, this daughter of Man

Inviting Us Forward

The noise was immense
The signal intense

Clear to those who believe
Invisible to those who still can't perceive

A world of beauty and grace
Living just beyond this place

Where color is sound
And the melodies profound

Touching the depth of our collective soul
Signaling to us the way to go

Away from the slowly swirling shadows
And towards the incandescent glows

Inviting us forward, just out of reach
Out of the past and into the breach

Building the bridges from dreams and sighs
Using our breath to answer the whys

Leaping and landing with courage and love
Drawing new strength from the stars above

Reminding ourselves and each other
We are here to reconnect as sister and brother

Onto the path and into the garden
Expressing our faith, asking no pardon

The flowers nodding their heads to Gaia's beat
Rising ever higher, curious to greet

These new seeds in their human disguise
Glowing with hope, fallen fresh from the sky

Our presence promises that life will go on
Joining all of Nature in singing Gaia's song

Praising this time, this place, this moment
Sharing our gratitude for the chance to foment

A revolution of beauty, a story of love
Carried to the horizon on the wings of a dove

Carrying the Divine Spark

Keep your eye on the sparrows
As you travel through the narrows

Carrying the Divine spark
Illuminating the dark

Graceful beauty as we fly
Over the chasm of why

Into the valley of why not
Where we'll find our spot

To root in the verdant earth
Activating the story of rebirth

Transforming into a blooming flower
Which holds the mystical power

To draw the butterflies from the skies
Hearkening to our hearts' cries

For hope, love and beauty
To fulfill our sacred duty

To fill the world with love
Reflecting the heavens above

Earthbound stars shining with truth
Offering abundant proof

That the story of future is hidden
Until the moment it is bidden

Revealing itself to the waiting world
Expressing the power of souls unfurled

To begin the ripple that starts the wave
Bringing forward the story we crave

Of love and peace and enough for all
In this story of rising after the fall

Moving Ever Closer

The surest way to not forget, is to remember
To experience the flame, stir the ember

Reminders of those who shared the story
Seen in the fire, glowing with glory

Those who see the truth of who else we are
We share each other's secrets borne from a star

Seen clearly by those who embrace the vision
The complexity of truth shared with precision

Each color discovered
Each thread recovered

Each word is heard
Every petal unfurled

The perfume inhaled
Inspires new tales

Of love and beauty
And the joy of duty

In service to the future we share
On the emerging path from here to there

Onward toward the glowing horizon
Moving ever closer, keeping our eyes on

The light of dawn focusing our sight
We gladly emerge from the endless night

Our truths are no longer buried
Laying down the burdens too long carried

Releasing the wisdom from lessons learned
Stepping joyfully into the future we've earned

Trusting in the Wisdom

Rooting deep and rising high
Discovering our how and our why

Surveying the world above the ground
Our souls awakened by what we found

The stars above lighting the way
Turning the shadows of night into day

The further we rose the more we remembered
Memories of future gracefully rendered

Within those designs the answer was plain
The miracles we seek are found in the mundane

No need for dramatic byzantine plans
We hold the key to the locks in our own hands

Taking a breath and going through the door
This land is an unfolding dream to explore

We expand our reach like flowers unfurled
Seeking the edges of this new world

To our surprise we find no boundaries

Instead there are illuminated foundries

The lead in our souls is transformed to gold
The traces of songs are now stories to be told

Alchemic magic performed with grace
Just one of the gifts of this mystical place

We carry our soul threads to the weavers
Each step demonstrates we are true believers

Faith guides us through the narrows
Trusting in the wisdom of the sparrows

Leading us to the light in the beyond
Where we add our voice to Gaia's song

Righting the Balance

Lean into who else you are
The terrestrial flower seeded by a star

Rooted in the Earth, rising to the sky
Deepening your faith that you are the why

Why a shared future has a chance
Why things can change with just a glance

Why what was wrong can now be righted
Why what was dark can now be lighted

Why the future is not the past
Why we are untethered, free at last

All of these whys have one answer
It's because we exhaled and became the dancer

With each twirl and grand jete
We see ever more and know the way

To reach the horizon in the distance
Surrendering to faith with no resistance

Like the flowers lining the path before us
We move with grace to the tune of the forest

Reconnecting with ourselves and each other
Rewriting the story of one another

Listening with our heart to Gaia's symphony
Fully engaged in our shared epiphany

The story of future is ours to write
Righting the balance of Shadow and Light

Showing the World

Which version is the you that nobody knows?
The authentic light hiding in the shadows

The one who remembers their life as a star
The one who dreams of who else they are

Sharing the stardust in thought and word
Dreaming of life as a bird

Free to fly high over the horizon
Tasked with the role of keeping their eyes on

The others hidden in the dusk and dawn
Who keep their cloak of invisibility on

But quick sparks of light reveal their soul
To the watchers who seek to know

Who is ready to join the chorus
Sharing their light to illuminate the forest

Deepening their roots in the welcoming earth
And rising high, expressing their worth

Out of the shadows and into the new dawn
Showing the world the story goes on

Exploring the Edges

Peeking around the curve
Her senses swerve

Into the future story
In all its glory

Her soul awakens in layers
Acknowledging the answered prayers

Exploring the edges of the world unfolding
Checking the map of the heart she's holding

The mystery of the past uncovered
Memories of future recovered

Each step on the path leading to what's next
Proves that she's passed an invisible test

Her heart, soul and head aligned
Anticipating the treasures she will find

Not measured in gold or gems
But rather in the blooms found on long stems

Purple, orange, pink, yellow and red
These are the fields of dreams in her head

Walking among them, inhaling the perfume
She is one of the flowers, a beautiful bloom

No longer apart from this joyful world
Rising high, her petals unfurled

Another flower in a flourishing field
Her true soul is finally revealed

Bending with the gentle breeze
She is a part of all she sees

Following the Birds

Sorting through the souvenirs
Collected through these many years

Disentangling from memories exponential
Still holding the hope of unexplored potential

Despite their gold and the worldly power
There is no escape from the truthing hour

We are all offered a moment of grace
Before we depart for another place

We are given a chance to unwind the story
Refocusing our energy to love from glory

At the edge of what comes next
We dance with joy, with no false steps

A last sigh before trying
A breath before flying

Off the ledge of what we know
Into the great wide open, into the flow

With a last glance back into the unknown we go
Into the Light, leaving the shadow

To the place with no up or down
Where at last the truth is found

That we are here to share our gifts
To celebrate each soul that lifts

Ancient stardust brought to the world
Shared by us, our wings unfurled

Following the birds to a new horizon
It's the small sparrow we keep our eyes on

Singing songs of joy and praise
We know in our soul that these are the days

We remember from our dreams
Lighter and brighter than we've ever seen

Over the forest and across the sky
Into the dawn of the new tale we fly

Following the Music

Silence has a sound
A truth waiting to be found

It has a unique feel
And the power to heal

Embracing the unseen
Allowing us to dream

Of other times and places
When we'll dance with the Graces

Following the music of the spheres
Listening to what a star hears

In the vastness the love echoes
Drawing light from the shadows

Reminding us that we are more
We are the place the wave meets the shore

The space waiting at the end of the journey
The crucible transforming me to we

This story is available to all
Where we rise with grace after a fall

Lifted by invisible wings
While the uncaged bird sings

The map of our heart unfolding
Inviting us to share the secrets we're holding

To loosen the tethers binding our souls
Following the music wherever it goes

Onward with faith that we'll find our way
Out of the night and into the day

Stirring the Fire

What is enough? What is plenty?
Is it a million? Or ten or twenty?

Is it a hundred sweet oranges waiting, unpeeled?
Is it one perfect flower in a field?

Is it the dawn on the day you finally felt loved
Or every dawn since then, is that enough?

You are valued by all in untold measure
You bring forward the hidden treasure

Sometimes it's hard to remember
But deep inside you have that ember

That quickly fans into a flame
Showing the world your true name

You are truth, you are love
You are blessed by the stars above

You are plenty, more than enough
An imperfect diamond in the rough

Music sent from the trees
Carried to us by the breeze

Stirring the fire in your soul
Illuminating the way to go

With your light shining out from deep within
Signaling to all the dance is about to begin

Releasing Spirits

A prayer for the dying
And those who are trying

To hold their hand and
keep it together

To bind their love and
loosen the tether

To be in the present
and remember the past

To celebrate the moment
that may be the last

This is the gift we are giving
To be there for the living

Until that moment of grace
When the transition takes place

Releasing spirits to what's next
To take the next steps

With the soul of the loved one
Holding us in their arms

As their story winds down
And we are shown

The power of love
That gift from above

Enveloping us in its power
In this final hour

The flower is losing its bloom
Sending the seeds to the loom

To become the fabric comforting us anew
After the soul joined the birds and flew

Back to the Source from whence it came
A worthy player ready for the next game

Sharing the Blessings

The kindness made her heart swerve
Throwing her theories for a curve

The fears no longer held sway
Over her reasons to leave or stay

For the first time in forever
She felt light as a feather

Her heart and soul unbound
As her feet left the ground

Following her soul over the horizon
Exhaling and keeping her eyes on

The shadow tracking her moves
As the story skipped the grooves

Creating a cacophony of sound
Seeking what needs to be found

In the new story unfolding
Rooted in the dreams she was holding

Deep in her softening heart
Eager to make a new start

In the secret garden of the ancients
Where the others wait with patience

To receive the mystical words
She had learned from the uncaged birds

Ready to sing the song of the future
Delivering threads for the weavers to suture

Into a tapestry of grace and love
Sharing the blessings gifted from above

Shining With New Life

Bent, but not broken
Whispered, not spoken

Inhaling the beauty
Of our sacred duty

To share the new story
Of the unfolding glory

Of the world remembered from dreams
The life far beyond the seams

Of the story to which we've been tethered
In which our words become the feathers

Our shadows and light form wings
Raising us above all those things

That aren't who we are
Dimming our inner star

Now shining with new life
Cutting the bindings with our soul's knife

Following the birds to the farthest horizon
Surrendering to faith, keeping our eyes on

The shimmering stars in the velvet night
Feeling their energy fueling our flight

Into the life beyond the shadow of doubt
To the places we only dreamed about

Where the threads of our story await
This is what's next, this is our fate

To gather the strands of what can be
To weave the story of me to we

Creating the cloth woven by the star and flower
Each twisted thread activating the power

To be and become as the stars ordain
To find our way to the garden again

Where we root and rise to play our part
And awaken the truth of our sleeping heart

9 789358 318944